On the Road to Patsy Cline

On the Road to Patsy Cline

POEMS BY
John Reinhard

Minnesota Voices Project Number 77
NEW RIVERS PRESS 1996

Copyright © 1996 by John Reinhard
Library of Congress Catalog Card Number 96-067818
ISBN 0-89823-171-x
All Rights Reserved
Edited by John Minczeski
Editorial Assistance by Carol Rutz
Book design and typesetting by Peregrine Graphics Services
Cover illustration by Gary Dougherty
Cover illustration inspired by a photograph by Leigh Marthe

New Rivers Press is a non-profit literary press dedicated to publishing the very best emerging writers in our region, nation, and world.

The publication of *On the Road to Patsy Cline* has been made possible by generous grants from the Jerome Foundation, the Metropolitan Regional Arts Council (from an appropriation by the Minnesota Legislature), the National Endowment for the Arts, the North Dakota Council on the Arts, the South Dakota Arts Council, Target Stores, Dayton's and Mervyn's by the Dayton Hudson Foundation, and the James R. Thorpe Foundation.

Additional support has been provided by the Elmer L. and Eleanor J. Andersen Foundation, the Beim Foundation, Bush Foundation, General Mills Foundation, Liberty State Bank, the McKnight Foundation, the Minnesota State Arts Board (through an appropriation by the Minnesota Legislature), the Star Tribune/Cowles Media Company, the Tennant Company Foundation, and the contributing members of New Rivers Press. New Rivers is a member agency of United Arts.

On the Road to Patsy Cline has been manufactured in Canada for New Rivers Press, 420 North 5th Street, Suite 910, Minneapolis, MN 55401. First Edition.

For Becky Colestock
Stephen Dunning
Dr. Eugene Haun
and my pal Leona Mitchell Reinhard (1901–1991)

ACKNOWLEDGMENTS

The following poems have appeared in these publications: "Rising above the Earth," "The Artistry of Pain," and "Living Will" in *Great River Review*; "Perhaps Our Parents Made Love After All" in *Passages North*; "Dad's Dinky" in *Poetry Motel*; "After Skinnydipping, the Old Couple Fishes for Brown Trout in the Root River" with Prairie Gate Press. Our thanks to the editors for permission to reprint here.

Earlier versions of a number of poems in the book were part of a manuscript that received a Hopwood Award from The University of Michigan in 1989.

There isn't enough space to thank all the people in the various towns who offered support to me and many of the poems in this book. Here are at least some of the names:

David Victor, Murray Jackson, Laura Roop, Kevin Walker, Mimi Mayer, Katie Maria Tassi, Andrea Beauchamp, Alice Fulton, Richard Tillinghast, Kent and Jane Cowgill, Gary Eddy, Kristen Twitchell, John Minczeski, C. W. "Wild Bill" Truesdale, Dan Eastman, Bette Lilla, and those students at Winona State's Residential College who literally camped out in my office and won't accept good-byes.

For helping certain of these poems get started, special thanks to Jim Harrison, Judy Flicker, Susan Walkenhorst, and Jill, Annie, and Calvin Raab.

Charlie, I owe you a Rolling Rock.

TABLE OF CONTENTS

I. First Storms

After Skinnydipping, the Old Couple Fishes for Brown Trout in the Root River	3
The Running Boy	5
The Artistry of Pain	7
First Storms	9
The Loneliest Road in America	10
On the Road to Patsy Cline	12
Elvis at 60	16
Places I Would Live	17
Clair on My Shoulders	19

II. A Way to Set Things Right

The Punchline	23
Cabin Fever	26
Jimmy Pohoski's a Woman Now	28
Perhaps Our Parents Made Love After All	30
Rising above the Earth	32
Fishing for Bluegill	37
"On the tip of the Tongue"	38
Last Ride down the Whiskey	40
Emily Dickinson's Ankle	42

III. Loss & Compensation

The Crazy Old Man from Faribault	47
The Private Parts of Animals	49
Learning the Names of All Things	50
Loss	52
The Death of the Town Drunk	57
Wyoming	60
Places Your Brother Would Send You	62

IV. Driving into Faith

Before and after the End of the World	67
Mortal Sins	69
Denise Robards Used To Live around Here Somewhere	72
The Newberry Chair	74
Dad's Dinky	76
Driving into Faith	78
Where To Find Heaven	83
Little Girl as Earthquake Lit by Stars	85
Living Will	87
That Night I Didn't Make Love at the Flamingo Motel in Long Prairie, Minnesota	90

1.
First Storms

AFTER SKINNYDIPPING, THE OLD COUPLE FISHES FOR BROWN TROUT IN THE ROOT RIVER

Peel back that thin top layer of the Earth's
skin and it might reveal a man
sitting alone in a diner
somewhere
on the Nebraska flood plain. Or
a woman flying
a kite in Arizona, a key
on her kite string to see
if electricity might find its thunder
on her blue
and cloudless day.
                    Or better yet
an old woman and man casting
elk hair caddis and blue quill flies
toward the heart of
a Root River pool.
They have their hip waders on now
but nothing else. They try to sneak
glances at one another, let
their lines float with current.
Possibly it was long ago
they came to this place
and first took their bare chances
with loving, scattered rose
petals on the caramel-
colored water and then climbed
down its rungs and on
to each other where they've stayed
enough years
for their own pools to grow
full and rich with swirls.
So it seems sudden

                        how
her rod tip bends,
a good trout on. When, finally,
she brings it to shore,
he bends down, lifts the fish
up from the river. They admire
quickly, as those
who have loved long
can, then give the trout back
to the place where its shadow has continued
breathing water and waiting.
The man kisses the woman's shoulder.
Her fingers flow along his chest.
                              On the shoregrass
pieces of clothing grow restless, bright rafts
unable to float
on their own.

THE RUNNING BOY

I'm envious of the way
his soft breathing strides
whittle the long field
down to almost
nothing.
           It is spring and he
is loping toward the apple trees
colorful and far enough away to be
their own horizon, sunset and dawn.
I wonder if I ever moved
like this, my body
a thin bird aching
toward sky, my sweat
cider sweet.
           Once the running boy
told me, "Even when I die
I'll run," and you can see
how he believes this
to his very knees. You don't run away
from death but through it,
death nothing more
than grass whistling soft
against your quick feet.
           If
I let the boy run much further,
he'll become no more
than a dot, a lost moment
of code. So I look around certain
that no one sees, then break
into a rusty trot.
           I ache fast,
my gut's bounce more rhythmic
than my run. I like

how my gut bounces, makes
sure I'm anchored.
                            But there's something
about this running boy
that gets me to at least consider
sprinting, about trying to catch
up, at least until my bad tendon
reins me in, says time to think about
that woman you love, her bum knee,
the gray already in her hair
at 29, time for a beer, to realize
you hurt and more running
will not help.
                    And now
the running boy is moving
very fast, small and large
at the same time, like Venus
on rare nights. Or beyond even that,
the dead star whose light
on a town in the middle of nowhere
still pours.

THE ARTISTRY OF PAIN

There is always enough hurt
to go around. She knows this.
She thinks it's not enough
to hurt quietly, that to proclaim
is to make less. So

the poet clears her throat, says,
"I would like to read from a series
of poems I have written about
pain." The first involves a man
who has lost the use
of his legs after being hit
by a truck. His boss fires him.
His wife leaves him for the man
who drove the truck. And oh he feels
"the pain, the pain, except
in his toes which he cannot feel
at all."
        Pain, part two, concerns a woman
eaten, but only half way,
by cannibals. She then must watch
as her husband is transformed
into the stuff of bouillabaisse, one
eye staring back at her as if plucked
from a sea bass.
        Her pain is endless
as a drive all the way across
Nebraska. And I leave it there,
dust smoking in the Wahoo fields.

Later, I call my mother, say, "Ma,
I just sat for an hour and listened
to a woman read poems about pain."

Ma says, "You're not
going to marry her, are you?"

My mother likes poems that rhyme,
end happy and neat as old movies.
My mother was pregnant twelve times, felt
four die inside her. She saw two others fade
only a few days into light. She wrote
in her diary that they were small
and the world was big. They lived
long enough to be blessed,
attached to a name, and buried
in solid ground. One more child
lived twenty-five years, remained small
in a big world.
                       My mother holds
my father's hand sometimes. Says "Piss"
when she's angry, and bakes an angel food
cake every Christmas for the baby Jesus.
She dyes away the gray in her hair,
sings country songs when she vacuums,
and drinks two Old Milwaukees every afternoon.

Ask her about her life.

She will tell you
her children are handsome, not ridiculously thin,
and smart enough to walk in the right kind
of rain. She is still in love. When she is sad,
it is for others whose lives
have not been so good. The ones
run over on dark streets, who do not have
the strength, audacity, or luck   to rise.

FIRST STORMS

The snow comes too soon
from the west, I think,
where once
before a blizzard
I saw clouds topple
off mountains
like heads off the shoulders
of French dukes
in revolution.

Last week was the one
that froze the river,
another old friend stone-
faced, logical
as calculus.

The snow moves fast
like dust into the attics
of all the houses
where we might have lived.
Dust
the library of every place
we breathe in, particles

of photographs and violins and
late afternoon rain and the small
hairs of lovers and words
whittled down
to quick, almost imperceptible
sounds. How soon it is

the storm takes shape
from one direction
or another, like jazz or dreams
and love, the white world
steps down at last
from its dark, close room.

THE LONELIEST ROAD IN AMERICA

We could've gone the other way, freeway
through Lovelock and Winnemucca.
Roads salted, highway clear all through
to Utah.
        But she and I took a turn
near Fernley, down
"The Loveliest Road in America."
Highway 50. To find beauty in such
spots as this is what rolls the dice
in the first place. The desert rose. Atoms
mushrooming out of the sand.
        The dry lakes take over
not far out of Fallon. Trees
disappear. The only building
is a whorehouse spread out
in the flats where small clouds that must be perfume float
like the smiles of Ohio salesmen who are faithful
to their lives.
        Twenty miles later we see
a second sign, realize *loveliest*
is actually *loneliest*. We are on a road
one letter of the alphabet turned sour,
and we're too far to go back. We have been swallowed
by Nevada, its women, and our own bodies,
which have wanted to turn to one another
and have not. Soon, summits not in the atlas
emerge from the land. The road ices
as it rises. Tires waver.
        We're here
because I wanted to take a woman
someplace right. We end up immersed into all
that's gone wrong. She is afraid
we are heading toward days more brutal

than the flats, grayer
than the peaks we slide across.
                              I pretend
I am older than her hurt. My hand moves to soothe
the back of her neck, as if this says
my hand will join with her
for she is lovely.
                    Even the land leans
toward its own odd beauty, chutes of wind
and silver and snake and sky.
                              And we drive
toward some unsigned stretch of road
where shade surprises, and colorwheels revolve
in the black fields. Where her sad neck arcs
toward delight and my hand
is still reaching. For she
is lovely, yes lovely, like me.

ON THE ROAD TO PATSY CLINE
for Sarah Dunning

1.
She could extend a note into a bruise.
I learned this long before I ever got hit hard,
long before I took a swing at anybody else.

When this life made me afraid
I was in the middle of a country
song a drunk would play

over and over in an empty bar,
I cashed in my change, filled my tank,
and headed out of prairie

toward Virginia where the hills
stoop like miners too many years
in the coal. I sang a thousand miles

of "Crazy" and "Sweet Dreams"
as Ohio and Pennsylvania sweated under my tires.
Then, as West Virginia began to rise like wings

I knew I was getting close
to something. Like a love you'll only lose
when you're ready. Or a perfect chorus

to that song you've been waiting
all your days to finish. Or a billboard
that says you've crossed the line

not only into Virginia but onto
the road you've been looking for,
where the sign tells you this

is the Patsy Cline Memorial Highway,
a shoulder to cry on,
a good road to ride.

2.
I first listened to Patsy Cline
in Muncie, Indiana, a place
where people waited for the ultimate
tornado that would lift them
toward Fort Wayne. Muncie,
where everybody hummed
through their noses, drank
lemonade too sweet
from Ball jars; where students
at the college named after those jars
demonstrated in support
of the Vietnam War, and I got beat up
for real and regularly by a guy
named Charlie Brown; where
Bobby Craig set fire
to grasshoppers and depantsed
his brother David every day
at three; where Kim Jones pointed
to the pregnant woman outside
Marsh Drugs, snickered
and said, "Y'know what that
means," and explained her
roundness, her two hearts,
her thighs like revolving doors
that would never spin for some kid
like me.

Not all of that fit
into a Patsy Cline song.

But late and great as she was
by then, she convinced me
I'd never be locked out of every life
that mattered, although
there were some sad stores beyond
the malls of Muncie.
I also learned no death
could stop a voice
from getting on the radio,
making boys and old men
sigh together like one long stretch of road
leading away from still-born towns,
from years spent waiting
on somersaulting clouds, the inevitable
storm.

3.
Myself, I'm coasting again
through Winchester, VA,
where Patsy shook free her voice.

I ate at the Triangle Diner.
Bought Benadryl at the drugstore
where she worked when she was sixteen.

Patsy Cline saw Jesus
in a nearby hospital
where he took her hand and led her

away from death for a while,
though he let her know
the plummeting was never far off.

From then on, Patsy swore
better than ever, shared bourbon
straight from the bottle.

And only two years
after walking with Jesus
she caught fire and fell from the sky

like a drop of rain
you might catch in your hand
if you were standing

on the right road, your own
Patsy Cline Memorial Highway.
Or you might get really lucky,

catch it in your mouth, swirl it
around like good whiskey
or a river
or a life.

ELVIS AT 60

He walks along the Cuyahoga River
humming "Don't Be Cruel" to factories
that whistle back in time and will not grieve
for him like sequined girls with perfect knees.
This river once transformed itself to fire,
actually burned its way through Cleveland,
leaving the pale moon to stare with desire
at something so quick to ignite, blaze, and
fade. He plays hide and seek with his own face
as it rises and falls on the Cuyahoga
like the notes that no longer have a place
to slide, no longer lurk in a sly fog.
So Elvis really has escaped the grave.
He's only in Cleveland, only alive.

PLACES I WOULD LIVE

Not Paris. Not London.
    None of the obvious choices. But
I would like to live in Riverton, Wyoming,
    near the Wind River Canyon
    where the water and wind swirl
    white with the spirits
    of Arapaho and Shoshone
    parting the earth like some holy sea.
I would live in Morris, Minnesota,
    because a shot and a beer's still cheap
    and farm women walk like
    they have some place to go.
I would live in New Zealand
    because there are no snakes.
I would live in Aspen, Colorado,
    if everyone else took off,
    leaving behind nothing but hills,
    trout, and one hot tub.
I would live in Gospel Hump, Idaho,
    because then I'd be
    a Gospel Humper.
I would live in Eden, if Eve
    came back, and the apples
    sang red, and there were
    no snakes.
I would live in Escanaba, Michigan,
    because the people there
    showed enough of kindnesses
    to bring me in out of the trees
    where I was sleeping.
I would live in Rebecca, the wild
    grasses of her hair, the sad road
    of her mouth.

I would live in many places
    with names we can crawl into.
Like Great Falls, Livingston, Laramie.
    Like Pierre and Menominee.
    Like Belle Fourche. Like Cannon Ball.
    Like Friendly River.
    Like Rebecca. Yes. Like that.

CLAIR ON MY SHOULDERS
for Clair Larsen

At four, she is fearless
of such high places.
"I'm taller than anybody!"
she shouts, to make sure
those of us so far below
can hear. And we walk,
the eight-foot hybrid
girl
man
until my shoulders
ache with song.

From here she swears she sees
Iowa, sees where snow is
rain and golden
grass, horses
feeding and running
fast as sun. She perches
on my shoulders as if riding
the branch of some ancient tree
where she can stare down
the old woman on the moon.

I knew my days when I was
the climber, not the tree,
though I never ventured far
from ground. I liked the
low branches of the small
apple tree beside our house.
My trick was turning the tree
into a tornado, allowing the storm
to lift me into its green

or blossoming belly where it
might ease a hunger while whirling
away my own unmoving ache.

When I tell Clair I was a climber
of apple trees, she is not
impressed. "You climb
anything else?" she says, so I point
to the old Highland watertower
and explain I climbed 175 stairs
to the very top. Clair smiles
at this, asks, "Could you see
the whole world?"

In truth, I could make out the points
where things just stop, trees
and rivers and good love
and the innumerable gifts
of eye and air. The whole world.

Yet Clair hangs on,
her small red shoes kick tapping
my chest where I begin
to breathe a soft
apple air that spins itself easily
around us, lifts us
for a moment until
my hands anchor
this little girl
and set her down
on the ground from which
we grow, always hoping to be
sturdy and tall and beautiful.

2.
A Way to Set Things Right

THE PUNCHLINE

Who can figure how we end up where
we are. Sometimes, maybe we're just looking
for the right song on the jukebox. This
is how I find myself at a bar
in Alma, Wisconsin, a Mississippi River town
made memorable by lock and dam #4
and by the power plant smokestacks
that are closer to the stars than any
two people in Alma. The Dam View
is a one-pool-table place with most customers
sitting up at the bar, ignoring
the initialed tables that say things like
"Dooley kissed Nancy's knee here, 1967."

It's been a long ride to Alma
and the Dam View where the only woman
in the place—other than the bartender—asks
whether she can tell a joke, Not really dirty,
she insists. Nobody says no. Besides
she's cursed every carom on the table on a night
when a lot of balls have been broken
and a lot of quarters lost.

I don't remember the joke very well.
I know that it had something
to do with mice, three male
and one female, orbiting the earth
in a wayward craft, not sure
how to get back home. One by one
the males lure the female to close quarters,
saying, Hey, I can get us back
to where the cheese is easy and the traps
are obvious. And when the female asks, How?

each male says, Stay with me tonight—
I'll tell you in the morning.

She falls for it every time.
If you're a male mouse in a bad joke,
this is perfect.

And if you're the only female customer
in the Dam View Bar, you go over
to old Leonard, a farmer with the life he dreams
he led written in blue letters
on his tractor cap: I HUNT HARD
                        I PLAY HARD
                        I STAY HARD

and just before the punchline,
you say to him, They make it
back down to earth, Leonard; it's a wonderful
ending. You wanna know how they did it?
Leonard's tractor cap hovers for a moment
over his life like a halo, one seed
not yet planted. Yes, Leonard wants to know.
You say, Stay with me tonight—
I'll tell you in the morning.

Who can figure. In this bar
there are forty songs on the jukebox
that never get played, not even
by mistake. And Leonard will go home
alone. And so will the woman
who told the joke. And so will I.

Now let yourself wonder, If there are teeth
in the very earth that will swallow us
do we let them gnaw at our bones even when
we should be singing. If you ask me, I say
move your lips. Find someone
whose knees you can kiss
underneath a table in a rundown bar.
If you want to know how to carve
this kiss in wood so it will last as long
as your lips can sing, long enough
for everyone to know that you
have come alive, at last, stay with me tonight . . .

CABIN FEVER

I know I should say, It's January
hard on the land's heels,
snow squalls and ice penning in
the lake and me. The problem is
it's June. Days
are calm blue while nights
emerge late and freckled with stars.

Yet I lock myself inside.
I've a window to look through
and beer and wood to burn.
When squirrels get physical
on the picnic table by the spruce, I feel
the fur on my arms rise, caught up
in their quick coupling.
Those mornings when I hear
Uncle Bill's ghost kicking
pine cones by the door
of this cabin he helped build,
I turn the radio up loud,
let the old warrior hear some
hopelessly out-of-step song
that sounds good to both of us.
Later, I'll watch the constant
waves, remembering how I watched
the oscilloscope
in Bill's hospital room, those waves too soon
flattening out into still water.

The worst case of cabin fever
I've ever had was when I lived
in a St. Paul high-rise.
I kept waiting for this woman

I was certain
would show up at my door
like spring, all garlanded,
all lilac and early rose.
Try living a while
alone in the house
of your own longing.
Think how beautiful and
horrible it would be to never
find the nerve to leave.

These days the rare storms
on Lake Superior seem no more
than a flicker of eyelash, a flutter
of straw on the great prairie.
Last night there was a rumor
of bear in the wind. And a howling,
the Chippewa war cries of
Uncle Bill's ghost or
maybe a timber wolf. Either way
I howled along until
the very voices of the cabin were shaken
loose, until even the wolf
of the body joined us, its howls
pulled by the heart's moon,
by the center of the sky closing
in.

JIMMY POHOSKI'S A WOMAN NOW

The tank arsenal was only a few blocks away
from where I went to high school. Sometimes
we'd watch the tanks maneuvering on their track
and we'd know this made us tough, our eyes
on steel, our hearts set on Polish American girls
whose names it took us years to say right.

Jimmy Pohoski, one of us, has cut away
what set him apart from the Chevy dealer's daughter.
Where he used to breathe out, now
he inhales. He gets fired by a boss
who can't decide which employee restroom
Jimmy Pohoski should use, Jimmy whose eyes
singed the sides of tanks bound for Vietnam,
whose dreams must've embraced the likes
of Sonya Banascek and Dixie Styles
on Michigan summer nights when
you would hardly sweat
and could kiss with tongues as though the sky
would never get tired of holding you up.

Maybe I should remember this differently. Say
Jimmy Pohoski never showered with the rest of us
after phy. ed. class, that instead he sat in the darkest
of corners, staring at that "thing"
and trying to push it back, down
and in like the finger of an empty glove.
But all I can really see is some guy
scrawny and ugly like the rest of us, hoping
it would be what we would grow into
that counts, and maybe still does. There
we were, surrounded by the tool and die shops
of Ten Mile Road, the auto plants of Van Dyke
and Mound, a war everywhere we looked
and no Dixie in our arms.

I was told, even then, that what we love
will leave us. It could be some moment
so dramatic as the long flight across
a sea. Or so simple as a short climb
out of our lives. In the old neighborhood
we'd gather at the Pohoskis' side door, all of us
yelling "Yimmy, Yimmy" in unison, figuring
we'd go and watch the tanks roll
off the line, all of us soldiers, none of us
knowing we could lose, or that boys could grow
to become anything other than men.

PERHAPS OUR PARENTS MADE LOVE AFTER ALL

He has grown lonely enough
to be in love
with the hills.

Late afternoons he climbs,
makes paths through
grass, mud, snow, wind.
He can see where
the town gives up
to swamp
and creek, gives
up to the river
that is, at once, always
entering and taking
leave.

When he was young,
he lived in country
that never moved.
Prairie had widened
into prairie. Mother
and father had
widened
into each other, into
their children,
into wheat and sky.

When he heard his parents
widening into their own
sighs he would hide
in the storm cellar, wait
for the dark spinning of clouds
to stop.

But from the tops of hills
he has learned
how every night
in his parents' room
there was death and
conception
and light breaking.

So now he looks
through his own years
toward days when his sons
and daughters will refuse
to hide from him
and the woman he loves, when
they will gather at keyholes
or doors ajar to listen,
to peek, to see how far
a kiss travels down a spine, fuses
to the flanks of the very hills themselves,
a little
something
of use.

RISING ABOVE THE EARTH

1.
She walks sometimes among the treetops,
moves her suddenly light feet across the high
leaves. She is in mourning for entire continents
being unfastened from the orbit of the earth.
And this is work. So she tries imagining herself
older than the rain in a place where fire
scatters from the sun to ignite each day.

There is an old country hymn she tries to remember,
"When He comes, if He comes, I will greet Him
on a cloud that is floating in the Word." But
who is this Guy? What is this Word? Cary Grant?
Love? Dancing? Fred Astaire? Sex? Sparrow? River?
She puts her head down among the leaves, hoping
they will say something, hoping that here will be
some trembling voice like God. When she hears nothing,
she decides to just hum the song, wordless as this tree
which offers her up so high,
and she remembers she grieves
for whole moments of the earth let loose.

Then she sees herself, a long time before,
on a ferris wheel at the county fair,
when the car reached the pinnacle of its arc,
one hundred feet high, and how it swayed,
part physics, part sky,
part something that for her went unexplained,
while a man below bought a ticket
and climbed on as she waited, suspended
at the very top of the world.

2.
Maybe it was 1970. After work
at the burger shack, some of us
would pick up a case of Stroh's that we'd sneak
down to the basement of my parents' house.
Normally, we'd shoot some lousy pool, lie
about who still wasn't a virgin,
and listen to "Don't think twice, it's all right . . ."
turned way down low.
                              But
if my folks were out of town
we'd crank the music up
loud like factory sirens summoning
new shifts, or girls' voices whispering yes
to everything we could imagine back then.
We played each electric song I owned,
lip-syncing the vocals, pretending
our pool cues were guitars, for hours
playing music that belonged
to someone else and singing with voices
that were not our own. When it was over,
we all looked to sleep and dreams
of women who breathed different
air than we would ever know.
                                      I'll confess
I played lead pool cue, left splinters
in my fingertips, singe marks
on the slick wood—seventeen years old and ready
to hit the streets. Some guys
my age tried to pretend
their pool cues were long arrows pointed
toward the hearts of pretty girls
or were rifles aimed at ominous trees
in the late light. Either way, they chalked their tips

and let fly. The poor bastards
could not conceive what it was

                                    to make music.

3.
All music or poetry or properly cut
stone is an ordering
of sorrow. A way to set things right.

4.
Not quite a year old, she really liked it
when I'd bounce her on my knee and play
Hank Williams and Ernest Tubb records
and tickle her whenever the records skipped.

I was ten and proud that I was big enough
to raise another human being right off
the ground. When she learned her first words,
"God a'mighty," I taught her how to say

"Goddamn," and she would sing along
to "Kawliga" and "Walkin' the Floor over You"
with all the language she had:
Goddamn. God a'mighty. Mighty damn.

Later, she learned mom and dad and sky
and bird and look how fall the rain
but the first words stay the longest,
work farther into us than all the rest.

When I was ten, I bounced little sister
God a'mighty into air that stood still enough
she almost floated, I swear, as if she knew
the very secret of flight.

5.
When she fell, it broke all of her.

Though I held out my arms
as if to catch her, I could
do no more than break
my own fall, hold only
to my own reflection.

When my arms were empty
even of that slight weight
I held
to the shadow sketches
of blonder days.

I held to Monet,
whose work she mimicked,
Who painted, she said,
like Hank Williams sang,
sadness blurred in everything.
Monet of the lily pads,
colors anchored
like rain
to the smooth water.

When she fell, I learned
to play four chords
on a real guitar,
my range no longer
unlimited, my voice
my own. And it sings

almost as hers did,
slim wings not much
to fly. Still,
"What a beautiful thought I am thinking,
concerning the great speckled bird.
The great speckled bird sits in splendor,
all surrounded and despised by the mob.
I am glad that I come to your meeting,
I'm proud that my name's of a bird.
When He comes, if He comes, I will greet Him
on a cloud that is floating in the Word. . . ."

FISHING FOR BLUEGILL

Way back when, I caught one nearly a pound.
Big eyes weighed it down more. My brother said,
"Nice fish," but sank his heavy line to bottom
for carp.
        No, we were not romantics then.
Whatever took the hook easy, we chased.
Say bullhead, rock bass, yellow perch, crappie.
Count ten, yank, and then pull that sucker in.

But even such a simple task as this
I found impossible. And bigger fish
like pike and walleye—or the brilliant trout—
were far beyond what I could do.
                      The catch
was that I could not fish without the snag
or broken line. I could not set a drag
or tie a fly or "think" like a northern.
It would've been simpler to fall in love
forever.
       I swore I'd go beyond myself,
dig trophies from the swirls. Go fishing blind.
But when my eyes opened, the line in flight,
I caught a tree. A fine, upstanding oak.
I left my grand cast twenty feet above
the ground and lake; the withering red worm,
the hook and bobber hanging like dead men.

I have been near water just once since then.
My brother, other family, and me
on a good-sized boat in a too small bay.
I hooked Uncle Bill Menard in the eye.

He swore he'd never fish with me again
and then gave thanks I did not set the hook.
My brother breathed deep, cast out beyond sight.

"ON THE TIP OF THE TONGUE"

On the tip of the Tongue
                 River, you are an
                         island
    and I'm looking
        for a place
  to land
     where the sand is soft
                 and the water
          cool to skin
               yet as the river
     laps at your belly so
        would I
     should the current
             and you
                           allow.

Not all that far from here,
Custer and the Seventh Cavalry
merged with the grassland.
And it is rumored that some
of the Oglala Sioux
cut out the tongues
of living men whose final words
were simply gasps
into the long twilight.

                 The river
          is just deep enough
   to hide
what I wish to hide
         in this spray of morning
      light
      and trout
          spinning

                                    toward
                                        air. I celebrate
                                    our tongues
                            and this water named for
        the shaping
                            of things.
                                And immersed
                            in the Tongue River, all
                                    of Montana flowing
                        by you and the river standing
                                    still, you
                                have become
                            a way of saying
                                something
                                    I
                                        have never said
                    aloud.
                                    So let us
                                listen to this river
                            that nudges wordless
                                                phrases
                                        to our ears.
            Let this river tell us
                                    we both
                        look fine
                                naked
                                    in the early light,
                                the sun being carried
                        gently
                                over the grasses,
                                    over
                                            the shore stones
                                toward
        the unnamed
                        but well charted
                                    territories of our skin.

LAST RIDE DOWN THE WHISKEY

So artfully do the Fates untwist
the threads of our life.
   —Montaigne

If herons spoke in ways you could
write down, what would they
say?
      I am afraid
of heights. Of the tickling
feather. Of blue
weather that washes our colors right
out of the sky.
              This is my
translation. In front of me
a heron scares a few feet above
river. The Whiskey's brown
from swamp creeks and soil
that would not stay. The heron
teases water with strokes of wing,
then lights a hundred yards ahead, always
solitary except in a few odd dreams
where I've seen the mass of herons, thousands
of great blues huddled on marsh, necking
like teenagers at the drive-in movies
before the cost of land went up
and owners went bust.
The herons mate for life. Then fly off
alone, one of them to guide me
down this river one more time.

Everything bends at the spear of land
called Widows Jump where wives remarry the spirits
of husbands who fell under the weight of trees.
My oars settle in whirlpool. I wrap it

around me for an instant then pull
hard at the river.
                        The heron leads me further.
The high water darkens. It was here
Père Marquette looked to the savage
for salvation. Columbus tried to sail
over the edge of the earth. And I wonder,
What death is it that kills us?
                        What is it
that makes us well? I've heard the land
is rife with cures. The healing scars
and trees that I could name like sons.
Medicine transmuted into stars that shiver
before me on the rutted water.
                        I have lived
most of my life and have little idea
what stays. I take a long drink of the Whiskey.
Let it flow through the channels of my veins.
Then I pierce the surface, once again hope
to propel myself forward to where
the heron seems to break through
the night on extraordinary wing.

EMILY DICKINSON'S ANKLE

Shitfaced at deer camp
we sit and toast to
eight-point bucks, to
too much red wine
in the venison gravy, to
the cool and lengthening nights
of autumn, to Emily Dickinson's
white dress, to the old farmwomen
of Nebraska who've turned to
poetry, to the way
love hangs from the human form
like silk and finally
to the human form itself when
Buck Lund offers up his glass
saying, "Here's to a woman's feet,
to the ankle and arch
and the way the foot moves
even when she's standing still,"
and Kent swirls his wine,
"Jesus, yes, there's nothing
more underrated, sexier,
than a woman's foot";
since these guys are hunters
maybe they fall in love
with what leaves tracks
in the snow and lets them
follow, and then Jane says,
"Men like whatever body
part they can get to
with the least difficulty—
this is not a matter
of aesthetics," Jane says,
so everyone looks at me,

waits, until I respond,
shitfaced at deer camp,
"I like a woman's smile,"
and the men groan and Buck
says, "You're growing soft,
old buddy. A smile? More
than breasts heavy with milk
or air or whatever
breasts get heavy with?
More than ankles? Red-tipped
toes?" and I have to admit
I almost said, "A nice fanny"
and thought of some
I followed for a while, yet
I never fell in love with someone
because I liked walking
behind her, while I've chased
women whose smiles
excited me, teased me close
toward something
genuine, broad, bottomless
as desire, and Jane says,
"I like the smile, too;
besides, have you ever seen
a man with nice feet?" Soon
all the bodies, shitfaced
at deer camp, give way
to sleep and forgiveness
and the various boundaries
of our delight.

In the morning's fresh light
the stags will bound
toward sky and some will not come down

as men pretend themselves
to leaves and burst
with fire, while I,
no gunman, keep long as I can
to my night's dream, this time
of Emily Dickinson, who leads me
to a small room
where she reads a poem
I've not heard before
of death and life in one
breath, and there
I throw myself at Emily's feet,
at an ankle
alone and too long sad
where I kiss her round moment
of bone, its poetry, her small
alabaster moon, and how
it shines, how it smiles,
how in light steps it gives
shape to one more
distant, tideless
landscape.

3. Loss & Compensation

THE CRAZY OLD MAN FROM FARIBAULT

You'll find him in this town
best known for its schools for the deaf
and blind. If you'll listen, he'll talk,
tell you all about the boy
who drowned in the Cannon River in 1958.
The weight of clouds
pushed this boy into fast water,
held him there until
the good Lord pulled him
free.
      Then the woman
whose death he'd mourned
it seemed so long. A love,
they'd made love, in showers,
on river banks, once
in the central fountain
of a Japanese garden. For her
he'd wept
vast tears, for this woman
who could tame bees, float
them into her palms. How
could he have known
that two years after her death
he'd receive a note, written
in her hand—he heard
the buzzing—
                that says
I thought of you today
It's been years when
I saw a flower bending
It was so heavy
With clouds.

                    He realizes
death is just a bad rumor.
And something easy as words
might redeem us. Soon
the notes will come, he figures,
from all the dead. Bring them
back from their long journeys.

Every day, hunched
beneath the clouds he hums
as he walks, back and forth,
in front of the famous Faribault schools,
places where the deaf put an ear to the wall
and the blind squint defiantly into dawn.

THE PRIVATE PARTS OF ANIMALS

The ad boasts of something called
the "Saco De Toro,"
a bull's scrotum
shaped into a sort of vase,
perfect, the ad swears, on a mantle
where it could hold a sweet bouquet, a sprig
of bent lilac. On a desk, ideal
for pen, pencil, straightedge.
By your bed, on a nightstand
it could provide safe keeping
for a few love letters
bound together
with ribbon.

LEARNING THE NAMES OF ALL THINGS

for Orval Lund Jr.

When his father takes him to the river
the boy at ten has learned
should the old man say, "Identify
that bird over there, just beyond
the spillway," the boy can say,
Cormorant, and almost always
be right. The boy has seen
the father drawn to this dark
and clumsy bird which to the boy
will always be a Dark and Clumsy Bird
That Fathers Seem To Like. If a finger
points far-off and says, How about
those migrating waterfowl? the boy says
Ducks if they look like soot, *Geese*
if they're bigger and slow
out of the chimney. The boy loves
his father, even calls the small red tree
Sumac, though to the boy it will always be
the Tree Full of Girls' Lips.

Those mornings when the boy hears
the persistant sighs that slide underneath the door
of his parents' room, he figures
this is how people cry out when they finally
understand the time they've wasted, trying
to learn the names of all things. And it's so simple.
Bird, flower, tree. Some tall or green or
skinny as a girl's eyes.

"The cormorant," says the father, "is also called
the coal goose." The son knows this is stupid
because he has seen a richer black vein of sky
formed by other birds. The boy has also eyed carefully
that girl who lives just past the fence, and he's noticed
how her hair is the color of cormorants
and that it moves with the same awkwardness
in flight. The boy knows
bird, flower, tree. Knows boy, girl. Knows
the sweet and small red tree that kisses your eye
and talks back to you
when you call it by the proper name.

LOSS

1.
This is the last song
Hank Williams wrote, on New Year's, 1953,
the day he died. His family
burned these final words, too sad
for the leaving. The ashes
took to sky, worked their way
well north until they hit the country
I was being pulled into.

The last song Hank Williams wrote
worked its way through
the Union Carbide smoke,
crawled across the fast blue canal
and down the shaft of my new lungs, breaking
into hard choruses of air.

Back then, I cried. Later on
I discovered how
you can collapse into yourself,
like Hank at thirty, the bones sucking back
the skin. Your whole being brought down
to three or four chords, a refrain
and goodbye.

The last song Hank Williams wrote
went something like the mutter of a wolf
that's lost its howl:

> Whiskey's smoother than any
>   love I've ever known
> It's loss that keeps you
>   rollin'

> Along tracks not even an ol' train
>   can ramble down
> Kiss my ass, pass the glass,
>   and I'll be movin' on.

2.
My grandfather was born into the last
song of Queen Victoria, which traveled
through prevailing winds across an ocean
to make its Marquette claim.

He never told us exactly
what Queen Victoria sounded like
to his Scotch Presbyterian ear
when she dissolved
into song. We could guess.

> Pleasure is a secret thing
>   Not made for brash parade.
> Love flies best on clipped wing
>   Light glows most brightly in shade.

My Scotch Presbyterian grandfather kept
Queen Victoria's last song in the safest
of places, in his left leg
nowhere near, of course, his thigh.
To be precise, he let it burrow
into a hollow just below
the knee. He never drove.
Never ran. He walked an even pace,
not far. He prided his life in quiet.

His one excursion into movement
was when he bowled. He slid on

his Queen Victoria leg right into
the Upper Peninsula doubles championship
with Harold Grugel, right into one absolutely
perfect game.
               When he was seventy-five, my grandfather
watched the doctors cut off his left leg
just above the knee. Almost immediately
he started hugging his grandchildren
and trying to pinch what he described as
the assembly-line fannies of the junior nurses
at Ford Hospital. The imperfect ones
he tried to kiss. He told ooh la la
stories about World War I. Said to my grandmother,
"I got a scar on my back—you don't know where."
He would live for one more year, developing a fondness
for brandy and the word "goddamn." A fondness
for smiles he could not explain. If I asked about
the days of Queen Victoria, he'd say, "Johnnie,
they can't send me to hell when I've already
got a leg up on heaven. Queen Vic wore her crown
at the wrong end; we all paid,"
and he'd let me sip his brandy, Napoleon,
before he'd give the hug that was always
the final one, both hands never less
than strong.

3.
The woman and I loved tiers of flowers,
full names, and bourbon alive in fresh mint
she'd harvest from the weeds.
We'd make up poems on the spot
as though it could happen like that
and stay. Her last letter said,
"You are with me

everywhere. Don't answer this.
Don't write back." For a long time,
I'd imagine waking, my lips tight
to her stomach, whispering.
Then the soft voice faded.
I drove across Crazy Woman Creek
and it was dry. I found
that the month of February
swells the moon though I haven't figured
why.
    Eight years later,
I see her again, see
she fits in my arms the same,
though not. When we kiss
we hold back our tongues. When we embrace
we keep our corsets fast. We save every poem
to revise. She's married now
and will not lie.
    Eight years
and we have each lost a sister, mine
to the death of choice, hers to death
out of the sky, a sister who
was knocked unconscious leaping
from a plane and never woke
to pull the cord, to make the fabric rise,
to use the air to fall.
    Eight years
and her mother has gone crazy into death
while her father felt his muscles stumble
toward nothing, toward the absolute where all
the blood she was born to has gone. And she
is in my arms where once we loved each other
to exhaustion, to bloom, and we can do no more
than cry ourselves not even to sleep.

> Whiskey's smoother than any
> > love I've ever known
> It's loss that keeps you
> > rollin'

I don't believe that, no matter
what Hank felt, no matter
my life. Still, it's something
I think of whispering in this woman's ear
at a time when "I love you" seems not right
and my arms can't form a single
proper shape. We move into one another
like remnants of cloth that soak up the shreds
of the moon, yes the February moon, as if we move
finally beyond the point of rending.

THE DEATH OF THE TOWN DRUNK

Make the town a small one. Then
you can be sure that Ed'll buy
beers every Friday, after work. Ed
blows up beaver dams, throws rocks
at wheat, was shot once
by an ex-wife. He quit drink,
but he buys.
           Other nights
you might go looking for Ray,
who likes to recite poetry from memory
when he drinks tequila, and what
the hell, you don't mind words
getting a little musical, even
some of them in Mexican and cactus
sharp the next day.
                Ray
could've painted the Stations
of the Cross once, in a small church
not too far out of Tampico.
The walls was bad, Ray says,
and the mescal was good. Get Ray
drunk enough, he'll say he's sad
he lost the chance of making something
people would've knelt to.

Back a ways, you and Ray
might've gone over to the Goodnight Bar.
Before closing, Madge from the credit union
would sometimes undo her blouse
all down the front, if you put your hands
in your back pockets and promised not to
talk cheap. Then she'd let you
inhale—your face that close—her perfume
sprinkled like gin on a rose.

So how many years was it before this
when you lived in the farmhouse.
You remember the big tub that you'd made
on your own. You were there
in the water with a beautiful
one-legged woman. And the snow in the hills
framed everything: the warm tub smell of cedar
and tar; the way her knee came fresh
from nowhere, the wood leg bobbing like a raft;
and how you climbed onto her, the water
cascading, a quick river
to the valley of her skin.
                            Then, too sudden
there's just you. The hills are gone.
And what's tough about level country
is that you can see how far you've come
to leave everybody else behind.
So one night, when Ray's out
after new things to memorize
and Ed's broke and the Goodnight's shy,
you scrounge a fifth of bourbon.
You walk out past the cornfields, past
Skunk Creek and the stumbling scarecrows.
Out to the flattest, stillest land
you can find, where new snow
illuminates the ground.
                          You feel, in this light,
as though you should lead some orchestra
if only there were violins or even trees
within a hundred miles. There are plenty
of stars, and they are close. Think
of your arms rising, baton steady.
                                   Oh,
let us honorably conduct, if not our lives,
the heavens we can see.

                              Let yourself lie down
on the white bed of a love that loves
only what it cannot see clearly
and turns blood to crystal like snow
that will never know the wind to swirl.

WYOMING

With each new death I push
closer to the prairie's upturned and fractured
edge. To places where a lost friend
has said the hills will make us well.
And whatever sickness is in me
believes this. Believes
in the spirit angling itself
toward the cowboy bars of Laramie
and straddling the high gray mare.

When I was almost ten I rode my only pony
in a smooth and tethered circle.
Over forty now, I dream again
the horses and their geometry.
I put my head into the gentle mouth
of grizzly. I outrun elk
into the white wind.

There are no people left in Wyoming.
Only a few voices that have decided beauty
is what we speak aloud when we're alone.
It was to Wyoming the last dinosaurs came
to smother themselves in blue air,
faded with nothing more than stars
in their eyes.

I have heard there are reasons for the rain
in Wyoming. I have heard not every mountain
has been mined, though there are churches
in Indiana that emerge in stone and light
raised from the Wyoming fields.

I am learning to believe what I can
about Wyoming. Its clean circles,
its proper burials. And how, in Wyoming,
there is more sky per capita
than anywhere in the world. Acres
and acres to stare at a night poked full of bright holes.
Here, more than ever, it is the sky
that gives us our imaginary wings. It is
the sky that leads us on.

PLACES YOUR BROTHER WOULD SEND YOU

for Matt, Steve, Cathy, and Dan

This doesn't speak to Abel's complaint.
These days, that would be easy. All over,
brothers circle one another
with spears, spill their own
blood.
        Last week, my doctor told me
I don't have cancer. The pain in my stomach
I must have made up, like some people
tell stories. That marble lump
is just
        a cyst. Everybody has 'em.
Benign, he said.

Right then I was sorry
I hadn't taken a handful of free
prophylactics from the bowl in the waiting room.
But I'd expected only a matter of time, had believed
enough in the pain I made up
to make up plans as well. The long drive
to a temporary cure of mountain and waterfall arcing
out of early snow. Quick glimpses of family.
Maybe five affairs out of the corner of my eye
with decent women shivering at bus stops
in Bozeman or Coeur d'Alene.
        Then the turn
not quite made on an icy road
steep in the Bighorns. The awkward final bow.
Benign, he says.

I go home, thinking
about imported beer, eggs with hot sauce.
At this point, my brother calls,
says he'll pay to fly me west for Christmas

with family. He knows that money's tight. Knows
how every absence leaves its mark.
                                              He can't of course
realize how easy it has become for me to love. That
I'm dancing the patterns of my apartment linoleum.
There is no sorrow. Just places to go where
your brother will send you.

He can't realize
how suddenly ready I am to walk open-armed
out into the world, how
for a moment quick
                        as a star
shedding its skin
                        I have polished my life to pearl.

4.
Driving into Faith

BEFORE AND AFTER THE END OF THE WORLD

When the fields finally thaw for good, the blunt
smell of manure is dabbed like perfume
behind the bending ear of our town.
Tractors emerge from hibernation.
The front porch thermometer reaches
toward sixty, and I'm tempted to drive
with Jeannie down a nearby dirt road
and impress our passion like gravel
into new ground.   Our son is learning
the curve ball. Our daughter has decided
she'll teach me how to move. First,
you boogie, Dad, then you learn to swim,
Dad, then I'll even teach you how to dress cool
and which way the corn leans when it's tall.

This is a town so small
nothing happens, not even the end of the world.
Jeannie will paint her fingernails
another color come Friday. The one band
in town will play echoes of old songs
that we'll dance to until closing, my feet
stupidly graceful, my arms pulling close
a woman of surprising colors. Life
simple and right as broken wishbone,
the lucky half in my hand.

On Saturday, Jay Feer will throw his famous
spring feast. Deer tongue, raccoon stew,
broiled beaver tail, and morels. Then more dancing
to oil lamp and sky. There is nothing
like this in Baltimore. No moon in Ohio.
Sunday morning, a little hungover
and heavier, I'll kiss Jeannie's left breast

which is also fuller than it was
the day before. Outside will be mostly
blue, say six or seven clouds to the east.
This morning the nets will go up
and I'll play three sets of tennis with Gremmels,
hit plenty of lobs. He's almost eighty.
I'll feel good.
Ready for anything.

I'll take him.

MORTAL SINS

When I was young in the confessional
I made up sins. Told
Father Donnelly I ate meat
on Friday, thinking it was
Thursday—but at our house Thursday
was spaghetti and Friday was
tuna casserole, always. Told
him, *Father, I let Maureen Carlson spit
in my mouth and I liked it*—but
that didn't happen
until much later, just before
Maureen moved off to Cheyenne.
Some sins I stretched toward
good. *Father, I wasn't as nice
to my brothers and sisters
as I should have been.*
I never told how I smeared
enough boogers in my sister's long
Hollywood hair that finally
she clipped it short
as a boy's and cried
for years. I never told
I went beyond spit, got naked
in a potato sack with my cousin
Wendy, that I once set up a flotilla
of tampons in the family tub.
Never said
I took my little brother down
to the coal bin beside
the Hansel and Gretel furnace,
pointed to the high coal pile braced
for winter, convinced Little Brother a man
was buried there, caught

when an avalanche of coal swept
through our town as it might
again soon and
Little Brother wept, put
a soft ear to the coal, hoped
he would hear it breathe.

I was going to be a priest back then.
The sins had to be right.
At least until puberty
hit and the early dreams got hard
as smoke.   I thought of this
a while ago when I heard
about the Pope's encyclical
and its reaffirmations
of the Mortal Sins: of masturbation,
of loving someone with inappropriate
parts, of coveting
your neighbor's wife,
of condom, of diaphragm, of
question.   Oh, Father, I am a sinner,
I am alive in sins, so full
I am already
burning.   Yet if you assigned
for forgiveness a simple rosary
I would shy away because
the rosary seems to me a bunch of dead bees
threaded together and I know
that dead bees can still sting.
Father, I lost my faith years ago
and when I found it again I believed

in woman, her body and
her holy ghost, and that I
could, indeed, respond in tongues.
I believed in Rilke's angels
rather than yours. I believed
in blue dresses that loved
the prairie wind, in old movies
where men wore hats, in small white crosses
which scale a mountain I climbed
myself one summer
in Montana.
                Father,
I believe that when you die
you become the body
buried beneath some pile of coal
come down like magic
and it's only someone listening
for your breath that enables you
to breathe back.

DENISE ROBARDS USED TO LIVE
AROUND HERE SOMEWHERE

I drive looking for what had been
the longest fence in town. Your father
leaning on the gate. You not far away.
Nobody lived next door.
                              You were the one
I loved first, Denise,
and it hasn't been the same since. Come back
as far north as I can go
to find you, I've noticed instead
that in our town the women
all hunch toward heavy. Tough from bruising
and husbands out of love, they wear
the weather. The men are fat, too,
tattooed in plaid. I'm not
all that thin myself.

Every street in town's been mine
at least twice tonight. Romulus and Remus,
the stone babies we used to laugh at
by the courthouse, still bite the tits
of mother wolf, our obsession with the moon
explained. The war memorial's been expanded.
The Temple Theatre burned silly the night
after showing its first pornographic movie.
That place where we watched Roy Rogers do good
without blood is just a vacant lot
wedged between the Flair Cafe and what used to be
Buster Brown Shoes.

Our town, Denise, has filled with fences
and they're all long. Some are white wood,
some are stone. Some are stacked

skulls and collarbones like stories
out of those *Official Detective* magazines
I stole from my grandmother and brought
to you with titles along the lines of
"Young Girl Feared Kidnapped for 30 Years
by Crazed Cartographer!"

Since I left here, winter hasn't been
right. And our town is drifting.
One way, across a river none can swim,
there is a country where everyone breathes
snow. Another way, my Presbyterian granny
is five years mad. And still another,
my grandfathers are buried in graves
my sister circles in delicate steps.
Denise, one way leads to you, whoever,
wherever you are. There are no maps
for this landscape. No more familiar roads.
No father out front to open the gate,
to say, "Welcome," to let us in.

THE NEWBERRY CHAIR

When he says, "Sit," I do, because
I'm company. And even the voice of the river beside us
suggests, Relax, in the only outside chair around
for miles. One chair for the trees to shade.
One chair for the wide northern sky to press down.
He stands over me, a dark cloud, tells me
wolves piss on this chair some nights
like putting out fire. Tells me
he bought this chair for five bucks
from the Newberry Home for the Mentally Ill.

Where I grew up, about a hundred miles east,
whenever I'd do something like stick a pen knife
into my cousin's belly—strictly a flesh wound
as I saw it—my mother'd take me upstairs:
"Next time, we send you to Newberry." When
I handcuffed Roseanne Fazzari
to our front porch and only a squad car
could set her free, when I
imagined out loud what Grace Kelly looked like
naked. . . . Hell, all over Sault Ste. Marie
parents needed only to whisper
"Newberry" to see their children suddenly
illuminated by the odd light of grace.

Now, twenty-five years later, here I am,
wondering who sat in this chair before I did.
Maybe some poor kid who didn't recognize
a valid threat when he heard one.
                                            At the state hospital
in Ypsilanti, there used to be three guys
who thought they were Christ and could save
anyone who wasn't insane. Perhaps there were Christs
at Newberry who sat in this chair, divided the lost souls

of the earth among them. Or someone
like my lost sister, who spent her time in the shadows
of Newberry; who spent her time in a place
that would not hold her, where she said
crazy people walked the hallways, fondled
the gray light. She would not be one of them,
she said, her smile crooked like a spade
about to cut through the surface of a dark field,
her smile the first piece of her to break.

My friend looks down at me. "You really needed this,"
he says. And he's right. But it feels good
to stand up, to lean against the smell of wolves
now rich in the air. None of you can explain
how right it is to walk away, leaving behind
some small piece of Newberry
carved out, at last, for me.

DAD'S DINKY

At the wake, Dad drank
wine from tall glasses.
Dad used to drink beer,
gave it up when Mom threatened to run
away with me, a baby then, to Toledo
where she'd never been, but
she and Dad both heard
that children and wives were never
recovered from Toledo
where back alleys
were main streets and rage
the one fire. At the wake
Dad drank wine, would not be sad
in a small glass. He said
Uncle Jim could give the eulogy
at the church, but no nun jokes
this time, not like with Gramps.
Jim said fine. Dad drank wine,
tall glasses. Said, If I gave
the eulogy or elegy or golly gee
I'd say my mother loved her children
because they were Irish. She was
going to tell us something else
but ran out of time. Dad drank wine.
Said, I love my children. They're Irish
too. I've lost forty pounds since Christmas
and I can almost see my dinky. Dad
looked down. Dad drank wine.

My born-again uncle Will left the room, went
upstairs toward heaven, while Aunt Grace
whose favorite word is "fuck" took off
her coat, decided to stay after all, to watch
Dad drink wine.

I have a friend whose father
saw a white unicorn gallop
across a sweet afternoon and three hours later
the man's heart gave out. So Dad looked down.
Thought, If I lose another twenty pounds,
I'll see Ireland, the rocky coast, that place
we come from. Another twenty pounds,
I'll see the tide scatter into stars, see
what Mother was going to say before she ran out
of time. Dad said, I've lost
forty pounds since Christmas, I can almost see
my dinky. It's worth the price
of admission. And Dad looked down,
tightened his gut, saw that thing, out of this world,
and drank long from a tall, clear glass.

DRIVING INTO FAITH

1.
Not more than two hours beyond Faith, South Dakota,
Devil's Tower thrusts itself skyward.
This is the twister that stopped
midstorm. Lifted the ground into chaos
and froze.
           The tourists
ask what gouged the tower's sides.
One guide tells them some earth goddess lover
dug her long nails into the land's humped back
and scraped to pull it even closer. Another guide
lowers his voice with his eyes
to tell how the tears of God ran down like acid
when the Power above saw evil
rise with such rapture
           while Faith
settled into the South Dakota dust, far
from the main road, far from any normal
turn of the wheel.
           In truth Faith was named
after the favorite daughter of the railroad man
who founded the town. A daughter who died so young
her father could only give her the roads he traveled
alone, a small town with a name large enough
to lay claim to the tears of God.

2.
We walked away from the funeral home in Grass Valley after giving my sister to ashes. Most of the day had turned on questions. Did we understand it was illegal to scatter ashes in California? Did we want a memorial notice? A Mass? A modestly decorated urn to keep above the fireplace? When we picked up her personal effects, the police asked whether we wanted the cord she had strangled herself with. My father talked to me then about believing. About wanting

a faith like my mother's that stiffens the backbone under the most enormous of weights. "I'd like to believe that way, I've tried," he said. "Maybe I'm too logical, but it just doesn't make sense. I'd still like to believe." We were standing in the middle of Gold Rush country, all the mines—even the great Empire—spent.

My father almost threw me out of the house when I was eighteen. He found out that for a year and a half I'd been walking two miles for a deli lunch instead of going to church. My mother calmed him enough that he said we could talk later. We never did. In a year my sister told him she'd stay home Sunday mornings and bake cookies. Soon after, my sister realized that my father was staying home, too, and she asked him why. "I've decided to go to Hell with my children," he told her.

When my father began to cry, I didn't know what to do. We had just let go what remained of the person most like us in the world, given her over to that other side neither of us believed. We stared into the mirror of ourselves.

Not all that long ago I learned that my father was the one who came to me most of the young nights when I wailed, the one who said babies aren't meant to cry. Not ever. This was the first time I ever saw my father cry, the first time he'd held me since I was a baby, the first time I'd felt his face like a rosary in my unsteady hands.

3.
Maybe inevitability isn't such a raw deal
if love's as inevitable
as death. A day at least
for the night we never wake from.

While I was in California, learning
that before love there is grief, Rebecca
drove the hundred miles south from St. Paul
to leave two carnations at my doorstep
and a note simple as a blossom

These with Love

I like the easy symbols. The two
flowers. The capital L of her love.
I saved the carnations until
they were delicate dust.
The note I carry with me
like a good rain, the kind
that skims treetops
and keeps everything green.

4.
The only miracle I've ever experienced
will not get me into heaven. One night, late,
I looked into the toilet and saw
a bat swimming. A green-black horny bat
extending its wings, not exactly
Gabriel.   I woke Rebecca up,
made her look. There were no windows
in this room. No holes in the floor.
(With miracles, you always have to look
for the holes in the floor.) Rebecca
was impressed. She didn't know then
it would be up to her when morning
showed, to stare at that miracle, give
thanks for the vision, the green-black wings,
and then flush it all back home.

5.
Next to the freeway, there were these two
signs, piggy-backed so they might as well be
one:

PREPARE TO MEET
THY GOD
Best Motel
2 blks south

And before I make my drive
to Faith, I put myself in a room
at the Best Motel, seven units, across
from acres of mall. The only other
occupied room is next to mine and, mostly,
all I do is listen in.
God's fairly quiet. But his breathing
is raspy, like a smoker's.
He loves his wife during the late news,
in between the weather and sports.
He snores doves and wakes early.
As he and his wife drive off, I miss
his face, but the car's American,
its license plate green and white
and brown, South Dakota.

6.
There are some lines I'd like to steal from
my favorite movie:

> "He didn't know when he first
> saw her. Or what it was
> about her that caught his eye.
> Maybe it was the way
> the wind blew thru her hair."

Rebecca says I want an always.
And I can never have this.

> "Give'm a flower.
> He keep it forever."

Maybe he loves how
she laughs
and he laughs
when otherwise he would weep.

7.
What do you say, Rebecca,
we spend our day in Faith. Rent
that white clapboard at town's edge,
the rattlesnakes outsinging the crickets.
We can tell each other the usual
jokes only we laugh at.
Mostly, we can walk, looking for trees
in this town of lost daughters
that is more open to the sky
than other places we have been.
And here, let me take your hand
as we go, for you I believe are
my resurrection and light,
such as that can be.
                                  There's something
comes alive in me with you
that otherwise is lost, like
the spirits that used to ride
through the Badlands, carving
stone with the careful chisel
of the South Dakota winds.
I'd like to walk into
those same winds, you close,
everything close in a place
where distance underlines
each motion of the eye.
I'd like to walk, you near
as the air, our day
exceptional in its clarity, one
hand toward another. A prayer.

WHERE TO FIND HEAVEN

If you're a gnat
you move simply
to the underside
of your mate's wing
where the shelter
and the updrafts
seem exceptional,
where you might flutter
at the entrance
to the cavern of
a cow's ear, flutter
until even the cow
begins to imagine the air
more musical than
the usual stutter
through tall grass.

Some time ago
my grandmother
from her sickbed
told the nurse to call
the priest. To call family close.
When the priest came,
she folded her hands
in final prayer, and died,
the air still as dust in places
where wind hides.
For my grandmother, heaven
was the rediscovery
of her lover's wide shoulders
as well as the new
voices of all the lost,
every root traced, at last.
Here, William Butler Yeats

could sing her lullabyes
for one sleep
that would never come.

Pascal once said
that a belief
in Heaven is a kind of Heaven
all its own.
He said this in French,
a language
I doubt. I doubt
the whiteness of frost.
The quickening
of our days. I doubt
that we are much beyond
our inclinations
toward more
solid ground.

But I like the notion
that Yeats sings us all
to a sleep
of waking. I like as well
the possibility
that a thing slight
as a gnat
might know the fullness
of this life. And that I
might fly somehow
beyond this flesh I am
and love
to be of heart and wing
the constant
fluttering.

LITTLE GIRL AS EARTHQUAKE LIT BY STARS

She is embarrassed by the steadiness
of adult life. Don't they know,
she wonders, there's a wind
beneath the ground too.
That birds soar through the roots.

When she was three she wanted
to be a field of yellow grass.
At four she was determined
she would grow up to be gravity.
Now though she wants to be
an earthquake. What unsettles us.
She will stop us from ever standing
still too long. A pacemaker,
like Uncle Jack's, but this one
for the heart of the earth.

Sometimes she dreams of meeting
the perfect boy, one with hair
like sawdust, one who will grow
to be a star. Not one of the greasy guys
in those movies her mother watches
in the afternoon, but
that real light that shines
across dark miles, something
measured only on its own terms,
by intensity and speed of flight.

Imagine as she does what a girl
as earthquake and boy as star could do
together. As if we might love
our own light enough to curl within it,
to fall toward ground that trembles
in anticipation of our landing. As if

light and earth could join and move
beneath us, jolt us into dance.
Imagine as she does what it is
to grow up and become rain or river,
symphony orchestra or garden, or one tree that stays
very tall no matter how far away from it
you go, no matter how high you climb.

LIVING WILL
for Leigh

1.
He wants to say,
This is how you save
yourself. He wants to offer
these words to her
like so many
small candles
in the dark back corner
of the church he attends
in memory.
                  He wants to say
This is how . . .
                  but then
he isn't so certain
what he means. What
earlobes these words
are meant to nibble on
as the syntax shifts
from verbs
                  to nouns.
Away from save
toward shelter, shoulder,
the moon broken in half
above a dirt-roiled field of snow.

2.
Unplug me if
the respirator eats and drinks
for me, cries for me
listening to Iris DeMent
or Emmylou Harris sing. Or if,
one day, you never return

from a late afternoon
walk.
          Should I be found
comatose
on a trout stream
forty years from now,

leave me there. Pretend
I'm only waiting for you,
that woman I saw once on the stream's
other shore, catching elusive
green boughs, pulling
my shadow as well, siphoning light
from half the moon.

3.
And when I give
away that shadow for good,
feed me to ashes
and let the wind hide me
someplace sweet
that you've always wanted
an excuse to visit.
How fine to be reason
for journey
          and not
the end of the world.

4.
But don't let death take me
to Indiana or Ohio or
any southern fields and towns
that line up east
of Texas.

            I know
Texas is dreary, too, but
I like the food and music
enough to be dead there, no matter
the winter chill of a Baptist rain.

5.
Better yet, don't let death take me
at all. That's really what these words
have been after. I want eternity
to kiss my way down the freckles
of your back, to rub your feet
after you and your daughter finish
shoveling snow. I'll cook dinner,
maybe ribs in sesame seeds and
red chilies. In time I want a child of ours
to climb out of your body's hills
and live longer than God.

6.
Maybe he could just offer her
fresh peaches. He imagines that nectar
swimming down her chin and
onto her breasts. He could offer
to lick them clean.
There would be that wonderful
flavor of peach and her skin
and even the taste of his own tongue.
Yes, that's all there is to it. He could
offer her peaches. Fresh peaches.

THAT NIGHT I DIDN'T MAKE LOVE AT THE FLAMINGO MOTEL IN LONG PRAIRIE, MINNESOTA

Only yesterday someone swiped it,
the eight foot tall
ceramic and steel
flamingo
from out front. This happens
every year, I'm told,
usually a local plowboy hoping
to impress
a farmgirl from Browerville.
Probably they ignite
a small fire in the shed stove
then sneak their skins beneath
the orange light of fire
and the pink light
of flamingo, probably
they pretend
they're in Florida, bare
to the edge
of ocean instead of
winter, flamingo song
imagined sad and sweet
as loon.
          A woman
with cornflower blue eyes
was going to ride a long stretch
of backroad to meet me tonight
except the snow, sudden,
closed her in, shut down
the moon cut way
to here. But she wanted to travel
toward my arms and by itself
that is almost enough,

        one journey at a time.
                              My plastic glass
half full I step out
of my Flamingo room
just long enough to catch some of
a sky splintered into snow
that will tame
my whiskey.
                By now
I'm feeling the wild
pure notes sounding off
inside me, as if they've
figured out how it is
not making love the first time
with someone you really love is
so much louder than making love
the first time with someone
you don't love, will never
love, no matter how
passion spreads through
your body like a rumor.
                               This not making
love is so loud that
from the room next door there's a tap
on the wall, asking me to
keep it down. Meanwhile,
the flamingo's gone, spirited
away, as the drifts gather like silk
around Long Prairie's ankles
and I'm closer to jazz
than I'll ever be again,
dark soil boiling
under the last of these
late snows.

© Clair Larsen

John Reinhard's first book of poems, *Burning the Prairie*, won the 1987 Minnesota Voices Project and was published the following year by New Rivers Press. He was born in Sault Ste. Marie, Michigan, in 1953, earned degrees from Eastern Michigan University and a creative writing MFA from The University of Michigan where he won a Hopwood Award and Cowden Fellowship. Teaching jobs at the University of Minnesota-Morris and Winona State University brought him to Minnesota; in fact, he is probably still there, somewhere, tackling whatever rewarding hack work he can find, and relishing the company of his wife, Chris, and their daughter, Quinn Maclean Reinhard.